RISE UP!

Revolution You.

A 6-step guide for personal change

RISE UP! Revolution You:
A 6-step guide for personal change

First published by Catalysis Publishing in 2018.

Paperback: ISBN -978-1-9999964-0-6
e-book: ISBN-978-9999964-1-3

See www.TheRISEUPguides.com
www.CatalysisConsulting.com

Dedication

This book is dedicated to my family who have helped me along the way. I'd like to thank in a special way Geraldine, Liane, Aoife and Elana, where would I be without you?

Acknowledgements

I'd like to acknowledge a couple of people who have helped me in the completion of this book.

Niamh who helped me get started on this project, Trevor for the advice when writing and finally Paddy, who kept asking me if the book was finished when we were out for a cycle. Thanks!

All the best!

Table of Contents

If you are vertical with a pulse then that is a great start to any day.

Jim.

Foreword

Alarmed!

The alarm on the morning of April 6th 2016 went off as usual at 6.45am and brought a new element into my life that stopped me in my tracks – for a short time. During the night, I had a minor stroke in my sleep. I got out of bed and fell but passed it off as my right leg still being asleep. I got washed and dressed and drove to work, still with my leg 'asleep'.

It was an examination day in the university where I lecture and as an examiner, I set up the examination room, hobbling around the table. The first student came in and It was only then that I discovered that I had immense difficulty writing, despite shaking out my hand several times (a typical male response to a medical issue!), I had a niggling suspicion that something was not right. I phoned my GP to arrange an appointment to meet him when the examination session was over.

I drove home to get to the appointment, but as a person who tries to be as efficient as possible, decided to stop at a shopping centre to pick up a new printer as the one in my home office had broken the night before. I made it to my appointment on time and walked into my GP's surgery.

My GP, Dr. Tony Cox, is a good friend of mine so I let myself into his surgery and walked into his office. Tony hadn't seen me come in as his back was to the door, so I sat down and we had the usual small talk and he checked out my blood pressure etc. Then he asked me to walk over to the examination couch and when I turned to face him, he had a concerned look on his face – he had seen me walk across his office. After a short physical examination, he confirmed that things weren't right and told me that I had the symptoms of a minor stroke. Not a pleasant bit of news to get at 4.00pm on a Wednesday afternoon! He sent me to hospital immediately where the diagnosis was confirmed.

Measuring my base-line

As a scientist, when performing any analysis, I would always take a base line measurement so I went about properly assessing my situation to see what my base line was. So here are the results that I found -

1. I could see – great!
2. I could hear – brilliant!
3. I could talk – fantastic!
4. I could think – what a joy!
5. My right leg wasn't working very well – not so good!
6. My right arm wasn't working very well – oh crap!

The latter two checks were performed in the cubicle in the Accident and Emergency department. As a 4th dan black belt in Shotokan karate, I could normally kick to head height and I had a very strong punch – however when I tried to kick, I could only lift my leg about 5cm and my foot was floppy, plus I couldn't focus my punch and it had zero power. That was when I knew for certain that I was in trouble and that the only person who could get me out of this trouble was me.

From A&E, I went for a brain scan (thankfully they found one!) it showed that the stroke had been caused by a clot and not a bleed which was good news. I was admitted to hospital and left to ponder upon my situation, and ponder I did while wobbling up and down the hospital corridor the evening after my 'attention seeking incident' as Geraldine calls it, we really value black humour in our house!

Background

I believe that everything is connected, so my life at this point is the direct result of the interaction of many factors. I'm from Northern Ireland, growing up during the so called 'Troubles" is where my resilience comes from. My qualifications and career have been in Science, up to Ph.D. and in Business, an M.B.A., giving me an understanding of logic, process and the need for maximising output from resources. Having run a successful business and lectured in a university, these gave me the experience of dealing with risk and transferring knowledge. As a 4th Dan black belt in Shotokan Karate, I know the power of discipline and focus. I have a sense of humour and try to find the funny in what I encounter when possible. But above all else, I am a husband and dad, the main purpose of my existence.

These essential 'ingredients of me' have all blended and helped me become who I am today in terms of my outlook and how I make decisions and approach problems. Now I was being tested and it was time to put all these 'ingredients of me' into how I would respond to what I was experiencing.

Active response

I'm a fairly proactive person, so the first decision I made was to move the 'stroke' firmly into the past and concentrate on what was ahead. I had had a clot in my brain. Past tense. By doing this, I could look at the process of what happened as both separate from myself and, more importantly, separate from now. This meant I had control in terms of how I was going to deal with the situation I found myself in now and not be anchored to an event in the past.

A couple of years ago I had read a book by Dr. Norman Doidge on brain plasticity titled 'The Brain that changes itself' and in it he had said that if a brain was injured it was sometimes possible to re-establish its functionality by taking a 'use it or lose it' approach. This was fundamental to my thinking on how to deal with the stroke, it had been described as a minor stroke so I took that on board as a positive and got to work on myself.

The scientist and business consultant in me developed the process, the martial artist in me defined the disciplined and focused response, the dad and husband defined the reason to drive forward. You're not dead until you're dead was my base line and I considered that being vertical with a pulse was an excellent starting point from which to move ahead.

Starting my journey

Based on what I knew about the brain, I immediately set about trying to re-awaken or reconnect the part of my brain where the clot had taken up residence and caused my 'attention seeking incident'.

I walked, not very well but I did walk, up and down the hospital corridor. My right foot was dragging a bit and my leg was heavy but it was moving and I wanted to keep it moving.

The morning after I was admitted to hospital, I bought the Irish Times newspaper. I can usually do its Simplex crossword in about 6 minutes, however that morning it took me over an hour, not because I couldn't remember the words, but because I couldn't get the letters into the boxes! A book of Simplex crosswords became my physiotherapy for getting back my fine motor skills associated with handwriting, with the task getting easier the more I did.

The practice of punching and kicking allowed me to try and assess any improvement in my arm and leg. So, I sweated through the process of rebuilding the level of function in my arm and leg. Every day looking for an improvement in terms of power, focus and height.

These were things and activities that I had full control over, I could do them by myself and I could feel and see improvement. The feedback was instant and didn't need any machinery or complex measurements – it was raw, visible and real.

Development of the thinking behind RISE UP!

As a business consultant, I was used to going into organisations where I had responsibility for developing, providing training on, and implementing solutions to, the problems they were encountering. I began to think of the various tools, techniques and thought processes that I had implemented in organisations in terms of how this knowledge could help me. This has led to the book you are now reading.

I've changed the tools and techniques around and 'de-businessed' them (no-one really wants to do an Impact Mapping Exercise on themselves) while maintaining the essence of the tools. They can be applied across all areas of your life where change is needed – your Health and Wealth, Relationships, Mental and Spiritual wellbeing.

The RISE UP! approach

There are 6 steps in the *RISE UP!* approach, with each step given its own chapter. The steps are:
- R – reduce
- I – increase
- S – start
- E - eliminate
- U – unload
- P – park

Each step will in its own way benefit your journey but when combined, the effect of each step is magnified as the activities create the space, energy, enthusiasm and belief required for the overall approach.

A word on the Own Zones

Throughout the book there will be points where an Own Zone is placed- designed to get you to think in a relatively structured way and apply what you have just learnt. There is some space provided to record your thoughts.
To get the most out of the book, complete the Own Zones as they appear and here are a few suggestions to help you get the most out of each exercise:
- Don't overthink your answer

- Go with your gut feeling
- There is no right or wrong answer, there is only your answer.
- Use the tools and thought provoking activities set out in the Introduction as required to help structure your thinking.

Visual Management

You are putting time and effort into reading this book so why not keep a record of what your thoughts and feelings are, the goals you are setting, promises you are making and the blockers you are getting rid of.   If you can record something and see it then it is more real.

Get a nice notebook and pen and capture your thoughts as you go through the Chapters and write down your answers for the questions in the Own Zones. Make sure to revisit and review them regularly and note any changes.

Sharing

Sometimes it is beneficial to share your thoughts and answers, other times they are best kept to yourself! Don't constantly look for external validation for what you are doing, trust yourself as much as possible while being open to help as and when you feel you need it.

So finally, take control and move ahead while remembering that the what, how, where and why behind your change is yours not someone else's.

Personal comment

At this stage, I have told you my story. It might resonate with some of you in one way or another. The rest of this book outlines the tools and techniques that I used to help me move forward. Some are really easy and some are quite difficult but I'd ask you to stick with it.

I got a lot out of the RISE UP! process – I've fully recovered from my minor stroke, I live a full, active and thankful life. I'm a different person now from the one I was on the 5th April 2016, hopefully a better one.

It's my hope that this book will help others, that it might be of some use to other people going through their own challenges.

 You've picked it up, now maybe it's time to pick yourself up. To *RISE UP!* and have your Revolution You.

Here's a quote to get you thinking!

> **We haven't come this far to be ordinary**
> **John Hegarty**

Chapter I
Introduction

Do it for you – a selfish approach

This book is entitled *RISE UP! Revolution You*, so it's about You. It may appear a selfish book but no doubt the improvements you can achieve through applying *RISE UP! Revolution You* concepts will also bring benefits to those closest to you. However, the only person who can activate and work through the *RISE UP! Revolution You* concepts for you, is at the end of the day -- you.

It will take some time and energy to work through the steps – time and energy that might otherwise be devoted to someone else's needs or wants. The requirement to focus on yourself might in itself be the first step in your *RISE UP! Revolution You*. Maybe it's the first time you have decided to *RISE UP!* for yourself and as such that might be a shock to both yourself and those around you – a good shock!

Take the time, focus on what is needed, work through the Own Zones and challenge yourself to look at you. Be selfish and see what comes out at the end. As someone once said – *be yourself because everyone else is already taken*.

Basic concepts that contribute to the process

The *RISE UP! Revolution You* approach to moving your life forward has a few basic concepts and tools designed to help you start and then move through the process. The remainder of this Chapter outlines what they are and how you might use them.

A word on Change

Change happens all the time, all around you and affects who and what you are. You can be affected in two ways, either as a victim of changes imposed upon you by circumstances created outside of yourself or as the owner of changes that you have created. For the concepts in *RISE UP! Revolution You* to work, you need to be aware of both sets of changes and make a determined effort where possible to become the creator of your own changes, recognising what is driving you to make the change, what you hope to get out of it and what can cause resistance to the change.

You have seen how change can cause disruption and discomfort, often jolting you out of the cocoon you have built, or have let be built, around you. Changes can be judged to be good or bad depending on how they affect you in terms of their outcome but often you judge the change based on how much effort it would take, paying little heed to the outcome. There can be a certain passivity when it comes to making changes, it's easier to go with the flow and trundle along as usual instead of getting involved. The quotation below from Barack Obama captures the outcome of the passivity and how the responsibility for changing yourself lies within you.

RISE UP! Revolution You

> **Change will not come if we wait for some other person,**
> **or if we wait for some other time.**
> **We are the ones we've been waiting for.**
> **We are the change that we seek.**
> **Barack Obama**

So, for a change to be initiated you must take the chance and push out of your comfort zone.

- You have to take responsibility for recognising that your current situation is no longer acceptable.
- You have to accept the discomfort and effort to make the change. You need to be proactive and move out of the victim mind-set.
- You have to start a revolution – you need to *RISE UP!* and start *Revolution You*. But remember, it can only start with you making the decision to start.

Permission

In change, the first action is typically where you decide to allow yourself to engage with the change – you essentially need to give yourself permission to make the change.

That permission can initiate any of the *RISE UP!* steps, but without permission nothing will happen. It is also true of the opposite in that if you decide not to change then you are in fact giving yourself permission at best to remain how you are, or, at worst to allow more damage to yourself. Never under-estimate the power of permission and the impact it has on your behaviour.

Behaviour is a Choice

There is no getting away from the fact that your behaviour is what has brought you to this point in your life journey. Your behaviour has brought delight, sadness, doubt, happiness and possibly clogged arteries from eating fatty food and not exercising enough! Every time you behave in a certain way it is down to a choice that you made.

Life presents you with situations and you then make a choice as to how you behave and the outcome flows from that. You have more power over your behaviour than you think, it's just that in the modern world it seems people have abdicated the power of choice to group-think or 'group-don't think' which might be more appropriate.

It's important to take back responsibility for your behaviour and to begin to reassert that you have the power to positively affect your behaviour and therefore affect your results. You've made the choice to buy this book, you made the choice to read it and now you must make the choices presented by the *RISE UP!* process to change your behaviour and get you to where you want to be. Behaviour is a choice – you can't escape that.

The 4E concept – looking at the Excellence, Efficiency, Effectiveness & Energy relationship

At this point it makes sense to say that there is no way to have perfection – it's an ideal that is striven for but it is always just that little bit out of reach. How you react to the 'impossibility of perfection' has a huge impact on how you approach your life.

You can just settle for what you have and live a safe, mediocre, not really satisfying but not really dissatisfying life. Or, you can really make an effort to be the best you can be, make the best of the resources around and within you to move towards a better life – how you describe better is up to you as there is no recipe for happiness!

Perfection is just out of reach, but excellence is absolutely possible and if you could say that you are living an excellent life then for most people that would be fantastic – it's almost as if excellence was perfection with a heavy dose of reality mixed in. So how do you get to excellence in your life?

There are essentially 4 key factors that you must consider:
- *Excellence* – what does your excellent life look like?
- *Energy* – how much energy and effort are you willing to put in to make your life as good as it can be.
- *Effectiveness* – are you clear on what the right things are that you should be doing so that you are moving towards the life you want to live.

- *Efficiency* – are you using all your resources in the best way to get the maximum return from them. Your most valuable resource is your time so deciding how you can best use it ensures that you are being efficient with your time, a foundation of the RISE UP! Revolution You concept.

By doing the right things for yourself in the best possible way you can move towards excellence and while this work uses up energy it will also create a positive energy that can drive you on further.

Let's not settle for mediocre and let's not push for perfection but focus on how you can make your life as excellent as possible. Not perfect, but excellent.

The Door

At this point you are standing in front of a door. Doors are strange objects in that they can be closed and locked to keep things out or they can be opened to let things in. The first choice you have to make is what you will open your door for and what will you close it against. The important thing is that it is your door and you make the decision.

Base-line – where you are now

The decision to start should be grounded in understanding where you are starting from. Deciding to change is just the start point, the transition to the new is where the work or journey really starts. The old adage that 'every journey starts with a single step' would therefore appear to be only half the story. The real start point for every journey is when there is a clear recognition of where you are now and of where you want to be in the future. Then the first step is a directed one, moving away from where you are now towards where you want, or need, to be.

This key action of recognising where you are now is composed of several things, each with a different level of impact and consequence, ranging from insignificant to either immensely positive or immensely negative. The start point is different for everyone and so too is the event that causes the realisation that where you are now is not where you should be or indeed want to be, followed by the subsequent drive to make a change.

So, realising where you are now is as critical as the ability to recognise why your current situation is no longer acceptable. Defining the trigger for the change, what drives you to initiate the change, is important. You need to look at what was your trigger point, the 'aha' moment, the 'Damascene conversion', the 'straw that broke the camel's back' to use a few clichés, that prompted your first step.

Own Zone Own Zone Own Zone Own Zone **Own Zone** Own Zone Own Zone Own Zone Own Zone

Some of the questions below might help to get you started in terms of describing your current situation or baseline.

Identify the trigger, the dis-satisfiers, that made you realise things are not what you want.

Identify the things that you feel are great, the satisfiers, and how you intend to use them to drive forward.

Identify what your main driver is to start moving away from where you are now towards your preferred future.

Drivers and Resisters

For every change, there will be drivers pushing you to make the change and realise the benefits from it. There will also be resistors there to block the change. If the drivers outweigh the resistors then you can move ahead and if the resistors outweigh the drivers then you stay or move backwards.

It is important that you recognise the drivers and resisters that can influence your decision-making process. Many of the drivers and resisters can be external to you such as the economy but many can also be internal – your personality, expectations, experience etc.

The identification of what is satisfying and not satisfying about where you are currently needs to be done and the balance examined. Look at both the satisfiers and the dis-satisfiers for the change you intend to make because when you look at the 'worth it' line, you may find that what you intended to do, could in the long run lead to a higher level of dissatisfaction. It is also important to realise that as you look at the change and begin to implement the plan, that the drivers, resisters, satisfiers and dis-satisfiers can change so it is advisable to revisit this as the change progresses.

When you start to look at the change you intend to make it might be useful to consider the 5Rs – these are important when looking at the Drivers and the Resistors:

- What are your *Reasons* for wanting the change? Plus, what are your reasons for not wanting the change?
- Are you basing these driver and resistor reasons on *Reality* so that you are working with facts?
- What *Resources* do you need for the change and have you got access to them? Also, what resources will be used up resisting the change?
- Are you clear in terms of what the *Results* of your actions will be?
- Lastly, but possibly most importantly, how is your *Resilience*, as discussed in the next section.

Resilience – your 'bounce-back-ability'

The *RISE UP! Revolution You* journey will probably not be smooth all the time – there will be bumps and bashes, false starts and failures, blame and tears. Your ability to be resilient and bounce back despite any setbacks you will encounter will have a significant impact on how you get on and what you achieve for yourself.

Resilience can be considered as the possession of an inner strength, a high level of faith in yourself and a good dollop of just refusing to be put down. This doesn't mean that you adopt a combative stance and fight everyone around you, what it can sometimes mean is that you have to fight against yourself in terms of refusing to give up, to take something less or believe something that goes against what you believe in yourself.

What can build your resilience early in any change is to look at all the elements that contribute to the change and go for the 'low hanging fruit', the early and easy wins that can produce a store of confidence and self -belief that you can draw on when things get tough.
The ability to set goals that allow for the early, easy wins is critical to your success, so here is a framework that allows you to build goals that help you achieve the change you want, while at the same time helping to build that store of self-belief as mentioned above.

Goal setting using the SMARTER model - defining your preferred future.

Setting goals is a critical action when looking at initiating a change as they set the direction in which you intend to travel. Effective goals are always written down and have a high level of commitment given to them. In order that the energy put into achieving the goal is not wasted, it is important that the goals be designed in a structured way. The framework that will be used here is the SMARTER goals framework as shown below.

The SMARTER goals framework is designed to allow goals to be formulated in a clear and concise manner. It is designed to make you really think about the goal and get it down on paper. The framework elements are described below:

- *Specific* – the goal needs to be described as clearly and specifically as possible so that there can be no room for misunderstanding. Once you have a specific description of the goal then you can focus on achieving it as it is a clear target.

- *Measureable* – for any goal, you need to know how you can gauge your progress – how far you have moved towards your target, how much is still left to be done and when you have reached your target.

- *Achievable* – the setting of realistic goals is vital to success. This does not mean easy goals, all excellent goals will have some element of challenge built into them. Being realistic but challenging would be two attributes of excellent goals as achieving such goals can prove to be a source of energy for you.

- *Relevant* – every goal must have a relevance to where you are trying to get to. Relevance can help ensure that you don't waste your valuable resources on goals that contribute very little to what you need or want. In many cases, you can fulfil the first three criteria in that the goals are specific, measureable and achievable but if you can't find the relevance then it is a poor goal. Relevance therefore is a filter that the goals must pass through before being accepted, resourced and worked on.

- *Time-bound* – effective goals have a time-line or else they remain as wishes. The setting of a realistic deadline allows for the planning and resourcing of actions required to achieve the goal within the given time-period.

Most people work with the SMART goal frame-work, however, two additional criteria have been added here that will allow you to create better goals.

- *Environment* –The first of these criteria is Environment and forces you to look at the environment you find yourself in when you work towards goals. It takes in physical issues such as space, financial issues, emotional issues, mental issues, fitness issues – whatever is in the internal and external environments that will help or hinder the work towards the goal.

- *Relationships* – this criterion makes you look at the relationships that must be in place to help you achieve your goals. It also makes you look at the relationships which may in their current form, block you from achieving your goals.

The SMARTER framework allows you to have goals that are focused on what you want and to base them in the reality you find yourself in. It should be noted that you can sometimes set goals in the wrong way, or even set the wrong goals– so you have to be able to go back and change. Goals shouldn't be considered as straight-jackets, they are just guidance posts along the road to where you want to be.

No matter how well goals are defined, there will be a few issues that could derail your success so it's probably a good time look at such issues.

Fear

Fear of change is a normal thing for people. You settle into your comfort zone, living and working in the way that has become usual or normal. The fear of changing this can be so great that the first step can be impossible to take, but as the book by Susan Jeffers advocates, feel the fear and do it anyway.

Some of the fears that block us from moving can be described as the fear of failure, the fear of ridicule, the fear of getting hurt, the fear of not being accepted, the fear of not knowing enough and in some cases even the fear of success.

> *"I have accepted fear as part of life - specifically the fear of change...*
> *I have gone ahead despite the pounding in the heart*
> *that says: turn back...."*
> *— Erica Jong*

Many fears could have a basis in reality, due to your experience or knowledge but other fears are only in your imagination, where expecting the worst possible outcome has anchored your thinking and blocked your acting. Therefore, it is important to be able to identify the real fears from the imaginary ones and to be realistic in terms of how you are going to approach them. In some cases, the fears can be very deep rooted while in other cases the fears have become a useful excuse to allow you to stay in your comfort zone -- you can do something about the comfort zone ones! Aristotle captured it well when he said:

"He who has overcome his fears will truly be free."
— Aristotle

Own Zone Own Zone Own Zone Own Zone **Own Zone** Own Zone Own Zone Own Zone Own Zone

Make a list of your fears and then analyse them based on evidence –

- *What evidence, hard facts, do you have that your fears are real and will be realised if you act?*
- *When there is no real fact-based evidence then why does a particular fear exist?*
- *How much effort would it take to overcome the fear and move beyond it?*
- *Perhaps more importantly you should ask what could removing the fear allow you to do?*

Own Zone Own Zone Own Zone Own Zone Own Zone Own Zone Own Zone Own Zone Own Zone Own Zone Own Zone Own Zone Own Zone

Interference

In sport, there is a formula for performance when coaching for improvement:

$$Performance = Potential - Interference$$

This is a powerful formula because it forces you to look at both sides of the equation – what lies within you in terms of your potential and what interferences are stopping you from realising your potential. The existence of fears rooted in your imagination can present a significant set of interferences.

Own Zone Own Zone Own Zone Own Zone **Own Zone** Own Zone Own Zone Own Zone Own Zone

You need to make a list of what the interferences are and where they can come from and then analyse them based on evidence –

- *What evidence, hard facts, do you have that the interferences are real and will come into play when you act?*
- *Are there interferences that are internal – that you have created yourself?*
- *What other sources of interference exist and what can you do about them?*
- *How much effort would it take to overcome the interferences and move beyond them?*
- *Perhaps more importantly you should ask what could removing the interferences allow you to do?*

Own Zone Own Zone Own Zone Own Zone Own Zone Own Zone Own Zone Own Zone Own Zone Own Zone Own Zone Own Zone Own Zone.

Risks and constraints

When looking at any change, there is a set of risks and constraints that need to be evaluated and a reasoned approach taken in dealing with them.

A risk is something that might happen during a course of an action or when the decision is made to take no action. The importance of the risk can be defined by looking at the chance of it occurring, the impact it would have should it be realised and how much visibility would you have in terms of seeing the risk emerging? This allows you to look at risks in a more open way and to be able to decide what level of risk you are willing to tolerate and what risks you need to focus on first.

When you know what risks to focus on then you can decide what to do about them:

- *Eliminate* – take steps to eliminate the cause of the risk.

- *Reduce* – take steps to reduce the impact or the probability of the risk materialising.
- *Contingency* – have a plan in place to deal with the risk if and when it materialises.
- *Surveillance* – keep watch for the emergence of the risk.
- *Avoid* – don't do anything that would trigger the risk.
- *Accept* – go ahead knowing that the risk might materialise.

Own Zone Own Zone Own Zone Own Zone **Own Zone** Own Zone Own Zone Own Zone Own Zone

List the Risks that you face when making a change.

Identify the high priority risks that you may have to deal with.

Decide on a way of dealing with the risks.

Own Zone Own Zone Own Zone Own Zone Own Zone Own Zone Own Zone Own Zone Own Zone Own Zone Own Zone Own Zone Own Zone

Constraints on the other hand, these are facts of life and you cannot get away from them, they are just there and you have to work within them. However, there are two types of constraint – external and internal.

Typically, external constraints can arise in terms of access to resources, abiding by social or cultural norms or within legislative limits – usually people have to live within the limits imposed by such external constraints. However, there are some internal constraints that you place upon yourself and that in effect you have control over. These are the constraints that you should work on first, for example – the constraint of low expectations, of your perspective of your own or other's social standing, of your qualifications, of your knowledge or of your relationships.

Own Zone Own Zone Own Zone Own Zone **Own Zone** Own Zone Own Zone Own Zone Own Zone

List the Constraints that you have when making your change.

Consider their impact on how you can work on your change?

Decide on a way of dealing with the constraints.

Own Zone Own Zone Own Zone Own Zone Own Zone Own Zone Own Zone Own Zone Own Zone Own Zone Own Zone Own Zone Own Zone

Defining your sweet spot and getting into flow

A tennis racquet and a golf club both have sweet spots on their strike surfaces. When the ball is hit by the sweet spot then the energy transfer and control are at their maximum and the player produces a beautiful shot in golf or a fantastic return in tennis. The sweet spot is where you get the best result, so, where is your own personal sweet spot? The components of your sweet spot might include – what is of interest, what you enjoy, what you like, what you are good at, what really gives you satisfaction. Usually when you are working and these factors are at play, then you can get into the 'zone' and the work just flows. For work that involves changing yourself, the more you are in your 'sweet spot' the more you can achieve. You need to be able to find your sweet spot and get into flow as often and easily as possible so momentum builds up and you start to move forward.

Own Zone Own Zone Own Zone Own Zone **Own Zone** Own Zone Own Zone Own Zone Own Zone

Describe your sweet spot.

How can you make sure you are in your sweet spot?

What can block you from being in your sweet spot? Some of these might already be in your lists of fears, interferences, risks and constraints.

Own Zone Own Zone Own Zone Own Zone Own Zone Own Zone Own Zone Own Zone Own Zone Own Zone Own Zone Own Zone Own Zone

Self-talk

Following from the last section where the concepts of sweet spot and getting into flow were discussed, now is a good time to look at how you talk to yourself. Your inner voice if it is positive, can be a fantastic help when you are trying to make changes. It can also be a great hindrance if it is negative. There are always plenty of people who will be more than happy to give you their negative opinions so you shouldn't be doing it to yourself. Henry Ford is credited with saying that whether you say you can or you can't do something, you are usually right! Getting your self-talk right is important, being mindful of what your internal talk is saying, gives you a clear understanding of how your self-talk affects you.

People generally like to be right and will always be looking for evidence to support that fact. So, if you are negative and think that things are not going to work out, you will be tuned in to catch everything that is negative just so you can prove to yourself that you are right! The same thing happens with positive thoughts. The good thing about this is that you are in control of your thoughts so you can do something about them if they are hindering your progress. You choose how you behave, and this applies to not only your actions but also to your thoughts and self-talk.

The necessity for positive self-talk can't be over-estimated. It's essential to your mental well-being and it's a key tool when you are setting out on a change journey. The caveat is that your self-talk needs to have a strong sense of reality and doesn't set you up for a big fall.

Own Zone Own Zone Own Zone Own Zone **Own Zone** Own Zone Own Zone Own Zone Own Zone

Is your self-talk mostly positive?
Is your self-talk mostly negative?
Notice how your self-talk affects
- o   *your energy level*
- o   *what you mostly notice*
- o   *your relationships*
- o   *what you get done*

Try not to do this in a critical way, try it in more of a noticing way, then think about what you can do about your self-talk.

Own Zone Own Zone Own Zone Own Zone Own Zone Own Zone Own Zone Own Zone Own Zone Own Zone Own Zone Own Zone Own Zone

Realism v Acceptance – Optimal Thinking

The ability to make the best decision based on what information you have is the basis of optimal thinking. Using optimal thinking helps keep you grounded in reality, while at the same time allows you to stretch yourself towards new experiences, opportunities and relationships. It has already been said that perfection is not possible but excellence is.

Examining your personal strengths and weaknesses

The funny thing is that when people look at making changes, there can be several that involve what you are doing, owning or relating to. To make an effective change, there needs to be an awareness of the resources available to facilitate the change and a clear picture of strengths and weaknesses. These can be captured and visualised by making a list of your personal resources.

Typically, the resources include the following:
- Time
- Energy
- Health
  - Physical
  - Emotional
  - Mental
  - Spiritual
- Relationships
  - Life

- o Business
- o Community
- Self
  - o Qualifications
  - o Experience
  - o Mind-set – self-confidence, positivity & realism
- Environment
  - o Home
  - o Business
  - o Community
- Experience and Knowledge
  - o Technical
  - o Social
  - o Personal

Targeting the effort – decide and do, influence, park (DIP)

Part of optimal thinking is to look at where the best return can be found when you use your strengths. This means finding the things that you can do something about. A lot of energy is wasted, enthusiasm lost and relationships damaged when you focus on things that you can't do anything about - even though they might be creating a lot of hassle and noise in your world! Acknowledge them but don't spend valuable time and energy trying to fix them. It's useful to look at where you have control and there are generally three categories:

- *Category 1: Decide and Do*
    - Here you have full control, you can make the decision to change, then go ahead and do what it takes. You have the resources, permission and drive to implement the change and receive whatever benefits are generated by it. On the other hand, you can't blame anyone else should the change go wrong as it is solely up to you!
- *Category 2: influence*
    - Here you don't have full control but can use your influence over others to generate the change you need. This can lead to frustration as often your influence can fall short of initiating action and things go unchanged.
- *Category 3: Park*
    - These are issues over which you have no control. Recognising this fact doesn't make them any less annoying, painful or costly and it's not about sticking our heads in the sand but it does allow you to stop wasting resources trying to fix things that you cannot fix. You have to recognise these issues and park them or put them in a box.

An interesting point about Category 2 and Category 3 is that as you clear all the Category 1 issues you may gain the space, knowledge, and reputation that increases what you have full control over, or it might increase your influence allowing you to deal with some things you would have had to Park beforehand. This means your DIP profile will change over time.

Have a look at what you are facing and list the things that you need to or would like to change.

Beside each item on the list – write in a D, an I or a P depending on what your level of control is.

For the D's - now you know where you can have an immediate impact, so maybe start with these.

For the I's – identify who you need to influence and how you might do this

For the P's – take note of them and move on. Recognise that there is nothing you can do about them – for now!

Avoiding paralysis through analysis

So far, there has been a lot of self-examination, thinking about why you should or shouldn't take a particular action, what people might think, how you might fail and what success might look like. Currently, everyone is living in the age of Big Data where companies are crunching huge amounts of information to make decisions that impact on their business and customers. Analysis is good, it's essential but it's not enough. Thinking about something doesn't get it done. You could analyse yourself and your situation until the cows come home but that won't bring about the change. The way you can make a change happen is to start to act. This doesn't mean that you won't return to analysis at some stage, in fact you most definitely will – but don't let it paralyse you.

Personal Comment

The tools and techniques outlined in this Chapter helped me to identify and overcome challenges that I met on my journey – both external and internal. Use them as you move through the rest of the book, maybe using them to help with the completion of the Own Zones. However, they only work if they are used!

I liked the idea of a space that contains your experiences and needs, as described by Kurt Lewin an American psychologist who came up with the concept of a life-space.

RISE UP! Revolution You

It's a concept that fits well with the aims of the *RISE UP!* process in terms of designing, building and protecting your own Life-space. It could include your mental, physical, spiritual, emotional, financial, work and relationships.

To create the Life-space that you want, start working on the *RISE UP! Revolution You* process, now! Do the countdown as Mel Robbins would say '5,4,3,2,1" and then blast off.

So – take a deep breath and let's go!

Own Zone Notes

Own Zone Notes

Own Zone Notes

Chapter II

R - Reduce

Introduction

There is a logical reason why I have included this section – I was too busy to do all the things I intended to do so I had to look at reducing some things to create space.

I found that as a first step the Reduce activity was very freeing and it allowed me to give myself the permission to remove some stuff, and people, from my life-space as they weren't positively contributing to my life. It was very hard at the start but once I realised the benefits, the Reduce process certainly gained momentum.

I can safely say that I have not regretted any of the Reduce actions that I took, in fact some were a bit of a relief! Have a read through the rest of the Chapter and see what Reduce can do for you in your *RISE UP!* journey.

Why do you need to reduce?

Looking at where you are, sometimes you can find that is hard to see the wood for the trees. Currently you are living in the age where you have gathered an incredible amount of possessions, some of which serve no function but just take up space. Take a quick look around and note what perhaps has been sitting gathering dust but you've just never got around to throwing it out. You've probably even moved it out of your way several times just to get at what you need. The same can be said for what occupies your mind and time, essentially your life-space.

At work there is a lot of effort put into tidying up your workspace during the biannual clean-up / chuck out before the holidays at summer and Christmas or just before visitors come to stay, but how much time do you spend decluttering your life-space?

When you look at it, clutter can be can categorised into a few zones:

> -Possessions
> - Personal space where you work.
> - Personal space where you live
> - Time wasters
> - Mind muddlers
> - Relationships

The basic questions are; what is essential in terms of what is needed and what can be reduced to free up space, or energy, in the six zones mentioned above?

Some changes look negative on the surface but you will soon realise that space is being created in your life for something new to emerge.
- Eckhart Tolle

Defining essential.

The last thing you want to do is to negatively affect what is essential, yet sometimes only by questioning what is needed can you start to define what is essential. To look at what essential means let's consider the following definitions:

- Absolutely cannot be done without.
- Cannot be replaced
- Adds or helps to deliver significant value
- Constantly in use
- Integral to a specific function, activity or role.

You'll notice that this is a very tight definition of essential and doesn't include words like 'might be' or 'always been'. Defining what is essential at this moment forces you to stop and think about what the contribution is or the value-add gained.

Since value is mentioned – it might be useful to look at what value is. The key thing about value is that it is different for every person. The value of a specific object might be extremely high for one person and yet the same object might hold absolutely no value for someone else. Value could be judged because of attributes such as scarcity, abundance, image, function, security, aesthetics, impact or benefit.

Own Zone Own Zone Own Zone Own Zone **Own Zone** Own Zone Own Zone Own Zone Own Zone

What do you think is essential in your life?
> *Possessions*
> *Relationships*
> *Activities*

Do you have a sufficient supply of what is essential?
> *If not, how might you increase your supply?*
> *Where can you get what you think is essential?*

How do your essentials add value to your life?

Own Zone Own Zone Own Zone Own Zone Own Zone Own Zone Own Zone Own Zone Own Zone Own Zone Own Zone Own Zone Own Zone

Our possessions -- The Law of Use

When you start to look at what surrounds you and gauge the level of requirement for these things, you can apply a set of criteria to allow a reduction to be achieved. The Law of Use is built on a set of criteria such as:

- When was the last time I used 'it'?
- If it was more than six months ago then can I get rid of it?
- Would I really miss it if it was gone?
- Does it still work?
- Am I keeping it 'just in case'?
- How much would it cost to replace it if I needed it again in the future?
- Does it still fit?
- Is it still in fashion?
- Is it an emotional or functional attachment that I have with it?
- How many times have I moved it out of the way to get at what I need?
- By having this, is it preventing me from having something that is better?
- Is there someone else who might be able to use it now and get some value out of it?
- What is the cost of keeping it in my life-space?

Own Zone Own Zone Own Zone Own Zone **Own Zone** Own Zone Own Zone Own Zone Own Zone

Take a quick inventory of your possessions?
Apply the criteria outlined above in an objective way – be honest!
How much can you reduce?
Could someone else benefit from what you don't need?
Get started!

Own Zone Own Zone Own Zone Own Zone Own Zone Own Zone Own Zone Own Zone Own Zone Own Zone Own Zone Own Zone Own Zone

The change in approach is from looking at things and thinking about what they mean and what they did for you in the past, to looking at the same things and asking do you really need them now? It's a much more objective way to view possessions and allows more functional decisions to be made without so much emotion. It is important to emphasise the fact that most people do have some possessions that have a very strong emotional link but no functional value, these things probably need to stay. The Chapter is entitled, Reduce, it isn't intended that you go off and dump everything! The following quotation sums it up-

> **"The best way to find out what we really need is to get rid of what we don't."**
> **— Marie Kondō**

Wants and needs - the Habit of More

In society today, there is a very materialistic approach to living, you could call it the 'Habit of More'. This approach may get in the way of your success, happiness and fulfilment by blocking your ability to define your core requirements. It's important to note that a degree of comfort should be built in when defining our needs.

As part of the focus on reducing what surrounds you, try to pay some attention to looking at what you need as opposed to what you want. This is particularly of interest when looking at what drives people to surround themselves with particular items.

Once you decide what it is that you need then you can ensure that there is space for these things and they are accessible as and when necessary. This does not only apply to the physical possessions or material objects in your physical space but also to what occupies your headspace.

"The more your own things, the more they own you" - unknown

Not everyone will have the same needs, depending on cultural, work, family and personal situations. What one person sees as absolutely essential could be seen as a complete waste by another person. Only you can say what you need and as this book is titled *RISE UP! Revolution You*, it really is up to you.

So maybe instead of reacting to what you want, stop and think about what you need, then make the decision. This might feel a little strange at first but when you see the positive outcome, this might become your default setting! The idea is not to become miserable by denying yourself constantly, but to reduce the quantity and improve the quality of what you have around yourself. You might even find that a drive to satisfy your wants leads to less satisfaction than focusing on what you really need.

Decluttering your workspace

In the same way that your personal space is cluttered with things that can be reduced, your workspace can have the same level, if not more, clutter. It's always amazing how you can significantly reduce the amount of stuff that has been on the desk for six months or longer when doing the pre-holiday clear-out!

There is the obvious decluttering in terms of reducing the amount of physical material in the workspace. The criteria can be applied for deciding what in your personal possessions needs to be reduced, looking at what adds value and assists your contribution and getting rid of the rest so as to reduce the clutter.

However, there is also a degree of decluttering that can take place regarding tasks and activities you are involved in. At the start of this section the act of reduction was stated as an intention to clear space and energy allowing your resources to be spent better elsewhere.

> *Clutter is symptomatic of delayed decision making."*
> *— Cynthia Kyriazis*

There are two key questions when looking at reducing the number of tasks

- What do you do that really adds value?
- What do we do that can be considered as low value tasks that are only blocking the availability of resources from higher value tasks?

It is very easy to be a busy fool and to focus on what you have always done instead of stopping and asking what you should be doing now.

The ability to stop and actively decide on what you are going to do next is a key skill to allow you to focus on what you should be doing, yet so many people act in a way that is passive with regards to where they are spending their resources.

In some cases, perhaps you work in this way because you feel that you don't have permission to challenge the ways things are done, or the way you yourself do things. In terms of reducing the number of tasks that block your performance or use up your resources for low value or negative outputs, you need to give yourself permission to make the right decision instead of the 'usual' decision.

This is the core of a proactive approach to work, focusing on those tasks that add significant value and being able to work towards your goals.

Own Zone Own Zone Own Zone Own Zone **Own Zone** Own Zone Own Zone Own Zone Own Zone

Look around your work space?
How much 'stuff' has been sitting around unused for weeks, months or even years?
If you reduced what was in your workspace what effect would it have?
Could someone else benefit from what you don't need?
Start reducing what is in your space – be ruthless!

Own Zone Own Zone Own Zone Own Zone Own Zone Own Zone Own Zone Own Zone Own Zone Own Zone Own Zone Own Zone Own Zone

The Professional No

People worry a lot about what others think of them and when asked to take on a job, keep on saying 'Yes' where they should be saying 'No'. Most 'askers' who get a 'No' when they ask you to do something, just move on to the next sucker who might say 'Yes'. That's the 'askers' goal, to get a' Yes' and dump their responsibility onto you. Once a "No" is received they have already moved on and they aren't thinking about you any longer – sorry to burst your bubble on that one!

So, people don't say 'No' because of how it might be interpreted and then after saying 'Yes", they go on to waste resources, especially that most valuable resource, time. The Professional No is the ability to say 'No' to tasks at this moment in time but to offer an alternative and is a useful way of safeguarding your time and improving your life-space. For example, you are asked to complete a task for someone when you are already overloaded so the Professional 'No' would look like – 'I'm sorry. I can't help you with that just now but I can give you a hand at 4.30 if that would suit?' Nine times out of ten, that won't suit them and they will move on without taking any offense. Try it and see – it does work!

Looking at how people act at work, there is a significant level of 90% Done Syndrome, where instead of saying 'No' to allow for the completion of a task, they say 'Yes' and take it on board immediately, stop what they are doing to do the 'new' job. When they return to the original job they had been working on before the interruption, they have to re-tune into it therefore it takes much longer, maybe up to 3 or 4 times longer, to complete. Using the Professional No allows you to complete your own tasks, reduce the occurrence of 90% Done Syndrome and increase your focus on adding value and getting more satisfaction from your work and your life.

Imagine what using the Professional No could do in your private life. Saying 'No' to the things that you don't have to do, that aren't your responsibility, that you don't like – but without giving offence. Say that you can't do whatever it is just now while suggesting a time in the future that would suit you. Provided you use common sense when saying 'No' you could reduce the amount of 'things' that get dumped on you.

Clarity – Roles and Goals

When looking at making reductions in terms of what is in your personal and work space, you need to have a clear idea of what the essential elements of your role are and to be able to protect them. This requires a high level of confidence in your own abilities, carefully balanced with a recognition that you don't know everything. You must develop a sense of flexibility and responsiveness to the needs of the overall intention of the business, or our own life-goals, to keep on track.

Working towards reducing the volume of non-value adding tasks that you engage in, means you need to ensure that when doing tasks, you have absolute clarity in terms of the end goal, timeline, resources available and why you are doing it in the first place. Being able to prioritise and focus, immediately reduces your level of distraction. Being able to see what adds value allows you to significantly reduce time spent on non-value adding activities and as importantly, to be able to justify your decisions and fulfil your role.

Own Zone Own Zone Own Zone Own Zone **Own Zone** Own Zone Own Zone Own Zone Own Zone

What is your role – at work, at home, in your community?

Are you clear in terms of what you do that adds value?

Have you got clear goals that are linked to your role?

Own Zone Own Zone Own Zone Own Zone Own Zone Own Zone Own Zone Own Zone Own Zone Own Zone Own Zone Own Zone Own Zone

Necessary evils

There are activities, relationships and requirements that could be classified as necessary evils. You know they don't add value and drain resources but at this minute in time they just have to be done. The consequences of not doing them outweigh the cost associated with doing them. In the last section of *RISE UP!* we will look at dealing with this in the form of Park – essentially park these issues and move on until the opportunity presents its-self to deal with the necessary evil and then decide to reduce it or eliminate it.

Reducing relationships

This might seem like a strange topic to bring up but let's explore it anyhow! Part of your goal setting activity using SMARTER asked you to look at what relationships have an impact on a goal or your ability to achieve it.

The act of looking at the relationships you are currently carrying and their value in terms of supporting you on the journey could be useful. It's not that you have to turn into a hermit, totally engrossed in your own little world, but it is useful to examine your relationships.

Sometimes, when you adjust your behaviour in a relationship you may be doing the other person a favour too. Some areas where reduction might work could be in areas such as where you are carrying other people's 'baggage', over-helping people so they develop learned helplessness or taking on responsibilities that aren't yours because you have always done so. Always putting yourself last is not a good position or mind-set to be in when looking at making positive changes.

Personal Comment

The exercises in this Reduce Chapter were challenging for me. The tendency to maintain the status quo and not upset the apple-cart by challenging myself, and sometimes others, was a big barrier. I found that taking a slightly more external perspective helped – when I looked 'from the outside in" I found that I was doing things that many times I had advised others not to do.

In the end, it was about examining what I had in my life-space and then realising that I didn't really need quite so much. Once I started to Reduce, my comfort in doing so increased over time and then I had to reduce my reducing!

Start reducing, but start small and let the process gather momentum.

What I'm going to REDUCE

No.	Action to be taken by me.	When will I start?	What will it Cost?	How will I do this?	When will I finish this?	What Support do I need?

Table 1 : Identifying the REDUCE activities

Own Zone - Notes

Own Zone - Notes

Chapter III

I - Increase

Introduction

I have always had the tendency to be enthusiastic and take on whatever came my way, without always making space for what I was taking on. By applying Reduce, I found that the act of increasing became easier and more considered. I was more aware of the impact of applying Increase actions as I realised their real cost, taking up the space I had gained by going through the Reduce activity.

This section looks at identifying what you need to increase to bring you to where you need to be. This starts off by looking at areas where an increase can be positive when the costs are weighed up against the benefits.

It is important to look at what you are Increasing and why. A balancing of cost to benefit as mentioned in the opening paragraph would be valuable as it would force you to look at the change being made, see the benefits that come from an increase in an activity while at the same time realising what the costs would be. This allows you to make an informed decision on the change.

Man tends to increase at a greater rate than his means of subsistence'
Charles Darwin

Resourcing the Increase

Available resources are usually limited, especially the time you have. It may be that by looking at what you need to reduce, eliminate or unload can release time for the areas where you need to increase.

A vital pool of resources lies within yourself and the ability to access them is a crucial skill. Applying these resources can start with the simple action of recognising what internal resources you have and then giving yourself permission to start using them.

Sometimes what must increase are these internal resources and some of them will be discussed in the following sections.

Auditing our resources

Identifying your available resources is a good starting point before starting to take the necessary actions to work on what you need to Increase.

A handy way to visualise your resources is to use a wheel chart as shown in the next Own Zone. Every segment on the circle is labelled as a specific resource. The next step is to determine what level of each resource you have and marking it on the target levels on the segment – the less of a resource you have the closer to the centre you need to mark and the more of a resource you have then you mark it on the target line further out on the segment.

The idea is to show what your resource levels look like, plus it gives you an idea of how smooth and how fast your journey can be when you join up all the segment scores to form a wheel. If your resources are uneven then you will have a bumpy journey, if they are all equally poor then your journey will be slow and if they are all scored highly then you will have a smooth and fast journey!

The greatest achievement of the human spirit is to live up to one's opportunities and make the most of one's resources
Luc de Clapiers

Own Zone Own Zone Own Zone Own Zone **Own Zone** Own Zone Own Zone Own Zone Own Zone

The template below shows the layout for the Resource Audit Wheel, take a few moments to complete it before moving on.

Own Zone Own Zone Own Zone Own Zone Own Zone Own Zone Own Zone Own Zone Own Zone Own Zone Own Zone Own Zone Own Zone

Developing your resources

Once the level of your resources is identified, you can clearly see where action needs to be taken to build your resources. The resources that score lower on the wheel segments are the ones that you need to focus on first.

The next sections will outline some of the typical areas where you might want to see an increase from your current level and how you might increase them. As you work through the Own Zones you'll realise how each resource may be linked and can be used for driving forward and building resources required for other acts of Increase.

Knowledge

To drive and facilitate the change that you need to make, knowing what type of knowledge or skills you need to increase and where can you get them is important. You must be grounded in reality, concerning your ability and have a clear idea of the cost and time required to attain the knowledge and skills.

Own Zone Own Zone Own Zone Own Zone **Own Zone** Own Zone Own Zone Own Zone Own Zone

Where do you see gaps in your Knowledge?

How can you increase the knowledge that you need?

How much time and effort can you afford to dedicate to increase your knowledge?

What cost is involved and can you afford it?

Who can help you?

Where and when can you start?

Own Zone Own Zone Own Zone Own Zone Own Zone Own Zone Own Zone Own Zone Own Zone Own Zone Own Zone Own Zone Own Zone

Network

What do you need to do to develop the quality and depth of relationships to build a great network? The ability to create a strong network of individuals who you value and who in turn value you, is a priceless skill that if mastered, or even better if it comes naturally, can give you significant advantages in directing and resourcing your change.

Connection and communication in an authentic way is what is needed, not the fake superficial 'networking' that is often seen going on where one person connects with the other only to see what they can get out of it. The ability to connect on a personal level and be of service leads to the development of a genuine network that is an asset and an important resource.

Own Zone Own Zone Own Zone Own Zone **Own Zone** Own Zone Own Zone Own Zone Own Zone

How can you increase the size of your network?

How much time and effort can you afford to dedicate to increase your network?

What cost is involved and can you afford it?

Who can help you?

Where and when can you start?

Own Zone Own Zone Own Zone Own Zone Own Zone Own Zone Own Zone Own Zone Own Zone Own Zone Own Zone Own Zone Own Zone

Open space

Open space can create opportunities that would otherwise be suffocated in a crowded space. Space can be created in your:

- Physical environment.
- Mental environment.
- Relationships.
- Time.

These constitute your life-space. The ability to create space is very useful as open space allows for:

- Greater visibility.
- More room for movement.
- Increased organisation.
- More freedom.

You should look at how you can create the open space needed and decide to build it into your daily activity.

What could you do with more space at this moment in time? Unfortunately for most people once space opens they then fill it with more of the same time-wasting, energy-sapping, claustrophobia-inducing objects, tasks, thoughts, people and relationships. To be effective, you should choose what you are going to put into the space and be happy with the fact that sometimes it's OK not to fill all available space but to leave it open as a resource for a future opportunity.

Often the best constructed documents or presentations are those that have the most white space so the reader can focus on what the important point is. Similarly, the most comfortable living spaces are often just that – spaces, and not crammed with unnecessary objects.

Own Zone Own Zone Own Zone Own Zone **Own Zone** Own Zone Own Zone Own Zone Own Zone

How can you increase the available space that you need?

How much time and effort can you afford to dedicate to increase your space?

What cost is involved and can you afford it?

Who can help you?

Where and when can you start?

What do you intend to do with all the space you create?

Own Zone Own Zone Own Zone Own Zone Own Zone Own Zone Own Zone Own Zone Own Zone Own Zone Own Zone Own Zone Own Zone

Self confidence

It is obvious that to make any change you must have the belief that the change is correct and the self-confidence to drive forward and make the change happen. How can you increase your self-confidence and self-belief?

Self-confidence starts with working on how you see yourself and in many cases, involves listening to how you speak to yourself. Does the little voice in your head help your self-confidence by using positive language or are you your own greatest critic?

Own Zone Own Zone Own Zone Own Zone **Own Zone** Own Zone Own Zone Own Zone Own Zone

Do you have a lack of self-confidence that is holding you back currently?

How does your lack of self-confidence affect you?

What is holding you back from increasing your self-confidence?

How can you increase your self-confidence?

What cost is involved and can you afford it?

Who can help you?

When can you start?

Language

The language you use determines how you perceive yourself and your situation (your internal self-talk) while it also affects how others see you (how you talk to others). The Own Zone below is focused on creating an awareness of the language you use to describe yourself and the events and situations you find yourself in. You need to look at whether the language you use is of benefit or is holding you back.

If you find that your self-talk is mostly negative, this means you must change your language so that you increase:
- The focus on solutions instead of problems
- The use of forward facing language as opposed to looking backwards.
- The use of positive words instead of negative words.

The power of the language used should not be underestimated, especially in your self-talk. You need to make sure that what you are saying to yourself is aligned with where you want to be and that it supports the changes you are making. Increasing the positivity in your language can have a big impact on whether or not you can see yourself as able to succeed.

Own Zone Own Zone Own Zone Own Zone **Own Zone** Own Zone Own Zone Own Zone Own Zone

Is your self-talk mostly positive or negative?

How does it affect your energy levels?

How does it affect what you pay attention to and notice?

How does it impact on your relationships?

How does it impact on what you get done?

What can you do to improve how you talk to yourself?

Own Zone Own Zone Own Zone Own Zone Own Zone Own Zone Own Zone Own Zone Own Zone Own Zone Own Zone Own Zone Own Zone

Energy

Energy is needed to initiate, follow through and complete any change so finding ways to increase your energy both physical and mental should be a priority activity!

Having a better diet and increasing your amount of exercise will help to increase your energy. Being around like-minded people and focusing on positive things will have a similar effect. As mentioned above, being aware of the language you use in your self-talk will also affect your level of mental energy.

In some cases, you need to stay away from 'energy vampires', people who seem to thrive on their negativity literally sucking all positive energy from others – you know who they are, so limit the time spent with them or if possible avoid them altogether!

It would be advisable to start slowly and work steadily towards building and increasing our energy levels. It's important to start with things that you can do, that you have control over, to build momentum that will carry you forward. The Own Zone below focuses on how you might increase your energy.

Own Zone Own Zone Own Zone Own Zone **Own Zone** Own Zone Own Zone Own Zone Own Zone

What's your energy level like?

Who or what builds your energy?

Who or what drains your energy

What level of energy would you like to have?

How will you get it?

Is anything holding you back?

Own Zone Own Zone Own Zone Own Zone Own Zone Own Zone Own Zone Own Zone Own Zone Own Zone Own Zone Own Zone Own Zone

Focus

There are distractions all around and many things that demand your attention so you need to focus on what you intend to do. Clearly identifying what must be done can increase your focus and help you set and achieve excellent goals or make and keep important promises.

The first thing to do is to decide what are you focusing on and then work on it. By setting goals some people will increase their focus, others might be better served by making promises either to themselves or to others. Whatever works is the one for you.

In the introduction, some basic tools for goal setting were explained, perhaps now is a good time to look at setting the goals or promises that you are aiming for. Increasing your focus means that you are putting your effort into doing what needs to be done. It makes it easier to say no to the things that don't matter and to direct your energy into what will make a difference for you.

In the martial arts, the term for focus is *kime*, the ability to focus all power onto a single point for a split second to deliver as much energy as possible into the strike, block or kick. The key thing is that once *kime* has served its purpose the martial artist then moves back to being relaxed but aware. This is a good analogy to life, you won't be focused all the time but if you can do it when required and then relax then your use of energy is much more efficient and effective.

Increasing your focus is also dependent upon how you deal with distraction. There are many sources of distraction in daily life – how long have you spent on the internet looking at silly epic fail compilations on You-Tube! This is time and energy that you can't get back so by removing or reducing such distractions can provide the room to increase your focus.

Increasing our focus, requires discipline because all behaviour is a choice. You choose how you are going to respond to all the stimuli coming at you through your screens, phone, conversations (internal and external), relationships, location and so on.

The bottom line is that you can increase your focus by deciding to do so. When this is linked to goals or promises then you have a strong chance to increase your focus and obtain the benefits that increased focus can deliver. But remember, it's not possible to focus all the time, relaxation is important, maybe through watching epic fail compilations on You-Tube – within reason!!

Time

Time is the most valuable resource you have. Time has several characteristics that make it valuable - supply is limited, it cannot be stored, it cannot be reused and it moves ahead whether you are ready or not. If you can increase the time you have available then you can increase what can be achieved and the only way to create time is to stop using, or more importantly to stop mis-using, it somewhere else.

In other sections of the book, you will look at what you can Reduce, what you can Eliminate or Start , what you can Unload or Park. By working through the activities associated with each of these with a focus on time, it is possible to free up time for what you need or want to do.

> **We all have our time machines. Some take us back, they're called memories. Some take us forward, they're called dreams.**
> **Jeremy Irons**

Own Zone Own Zone Own Zone Own Zone **Own Zone** Own Zone Own Zone Own Zone Own Zone

What are the main time wasters that you have?

How much time is lost to them – daily, weekly, monthly?

What is the cost to you of these time wasters?

Which time wasters can you easily remove?

If you had more time what could you do?

Health

Your health is your wealth – an old but very true saying. The ability to positively impact your health can lead to a healthier and happier life. The responsibility for your health lies with you – it's not your doctor or chiropractor or acupuncturist who has responsibility for your health, it's you.

Increasing your level of health may require lifestyle changes such as taking exercise, eating a balanced diet, cutting down on alcohol and smoking. As with the resource audit, it might be useful to do a health audit to build a picture of what your health looks like.

Alternatively, you could go to your doctor and get a health check, this is probably advisable before starting on a health program if you have any health issues.

Time and health are two precious assets that we don't recognise and appreciate until they have been depleted
Denis Waitley

The answers on how to increase your health are well beyond the purpose of this book. However, the questions relating to where you are now and where you would like to be in terms of increasing your level of health are relevant and form the basis of the following Own Zone.

Own Zone Own Zone Own Zone Own Zone **Own Zone** Own Zone Own Zone Own Zone Own Zone

How would you assess your level of health?

Is your level of health holding you back?

What can you do to improve your health?

Who or what can help you do this?

Can you afford not to improve your health?

What is stopping you from starting now?

Own Zone Own Zone Own Zone Own Zone Own Zone Own Zone Own Zone Own Zone Own Zone Own Zone Own Zone Own Zone Own Zone

Finances

There are many resources available to show you how to increase your wealth, so have a look at them and see if you can development a wealth-increase plan. A discussion with a qualified (and maybe recommended!!!) financial advisor might be useful in this regard to get some professional advice on your finances.

> **Rule No. 1: Never Lose money.**
> **Rule No. 2: Never forget Rule No. 1**
> **Warren Buffett**

However, it might be useful to list out where your money is coming from and where it is going. Then identifying where it might be wasted, or not giving you the value it should. As mentioned above – talk to someone who knows about finances and then follow their advice.

Personal Comment

When I focused on Increasing the things that add value to my life-space and facilitate my own *RISE UP! Revolution You* journey, I paused and thought about what to Increase, instead of just loading myself with un-necessary things.

To help sort through and make decisions on what I was increasing I used the following criteria and found them helpful.

- Increase what matters.
- Increase what means something to me.
- Increase what I like or love.

In other words, I tried to Increase what I could that would bring the most benefit into my life-space and to do so with a real sense of gratitude, not entitlement.

What I'm going to INCREASE

No.	Action to be taken by me.	When will I start?	What will it Cost?	How will I do this?	When will I finish this?	What Support do I need?

Table 2: Identifying the INCREASE activities

Own Zone - Notes

Own Zone- Notes

Chapter IV

S - Start

Introduction

I've always found starting to be easy – starting an exercise program, starting a diet, starting a new book. The difficulty was in a lot of cases finishing what I started because I had so much going on and I kept on adding to my load!

I then began to look at what I was starting and why. Becoming more selective when given the opportunity or having the urge to Start meant that I was making better choices so the chance of finishing was increased. Plus, by using Reduce or Eliminate (Chapter 5 covers this) I had more life-space in which to work on what I started.

In this section, you will be asked to look at what you need, or want, to start doing as part of your change. It might seem strange that Start is the third element of the RISE-UP process. Typically, when a change is discussed the first thing most people do is to begin to list all the things that they think need to be started – even though they are already overloaded with activities and commitments! No wonder so many changes fail.

However, having already looked at what you are going to Reduce, hopefully you have created some space to accommodate the things you are to Start. Plus, you have already looked at what you are doing that you need to Increase and this should be giving you some of the necessary resources to support what you are to Start.

Start is all about behaviours.

You have full control over your behaviour, it's a choice you make. Being aware of what you intend to start and why, allows you to focus on getting the right start supported by the right behaviours. This section of *RISE UP! Revolution You* focuses on getting you to think about the behaviours that you need to Start to support your change. The Own Zones are designed to guide you through the thought process, so make sure you take the time to complete them.

Start STOPPING

This might seem to be a strange starting point, to Start Stopping, but it is built around a set of actions that will be useful as a base for everything else that follows in this chapter.

- **S**top – How many times a day do you completely stop? Most people never stop, they are in continuous motion, physically and mentally. They are very busy all the time, constantly on the go. But the question is, how productive are they? How focussed are they? Think about your own day, how often do you stop? How productive are you? Why do you not stop? You must realise that there are significant benefits that come from being able to stop – not least the ability to decide what you are going to do next.

- **T**hink – this is about being proactive (you make things happen) as opposed to reactive (you have things happen to you). How much time during the day do you stop to think or are you too busy? When was the last time you thought about what you are doing? Are you on autopilot or have you abdicated control to someone else?

- **O**rganise – by being organised, you are more productive and you can get much more done. Good scheduling and resourcing what you are doing leads to better results. How well organised would you say you are?

- **P**lan – what's your plan? Do you have one? In many cases people are moving blindly ahead because they have never stopped, never really thought about what they are doing and why? This kind of unplanned reactive life-style carries with it stress, frustration, poor relationships, dissatisfaction and in many cases poor health. A bit of planning might bring great benefits!

- **P**roceed – move ahead once you know where you are going and why. It's important to get the balance right between thinking, planning and proceeding. Many people are caught in the Proceed stage, just doing 'stuff' all the time in a mindless way, perhaps through poor habits, lack of self-confidence, lack of knowledge or fear. They run the risk of being busy fools! The *RISE UP!* process is designed help you to proceed, but in a focused and guided way.

- **I**mprove – there is no point doing the same things over and over again, you need to be learning and improving. This is linked in with the Think and Organise aspects as outlined above.
- **N**otice – being aware of what you are doing and not just doing it. This brings in the concept of mindfulness, of paying attention to what you are doing and noticing the effect.
- **G**row – if you can start STOPPING then it is only natural that you will grow. All the above steps lead to growth of knowledge, productivity, confidence and success.

Hopefully at this stage you will see the benefits that can come when you start stopping. The Own Zone below will help to concentrate your thoughts on the steps involved in STOPPING.

Own Zone Own Zone Own Zone Own Zone **Own Zone** Own Zone Own Zone Own Zone Own Zone

Look at how you can build STOPPING into your life.

What benefits would you gain?

What will it cost you in terms of time?

Own Zone Own Zone Own Zone Own Zone Own Zone Own Zone Own Zone Own Zone Own Zone Own Zone Own Zone Own Zone Own Zone

Start to Start

The saying that the even the longest journey starts with a single step is a good one and is very relevant to the thinking behind *RISE UP!* A more insightful and appropriate one might be:

> **'Start where you are. Use what you have.**
> **Do what you can.'**
> **Arthur Ashe**

Often it is taking that first step from where you are to get moving with what you have now that makes the difference in terms of getting to where you want to be.

Starting to Start can fall foul of a couple of things that you do to sabotage yourself. For instance, don't say that you will try to start, be definite and say that you are Starting. Don't procrastinate and say you will start later – start now.

The advertising guru, Dave Trott says that *'If we can learn to ignore ourselves, we can do anything we want.'* Oftentimes we just need to get out of our own way and make the start.

There is always fear when you are about to make a change so make sure that you start small and get small wins. These build your confidence and credibility and will lead on to bigger wins. The only way to get the benefit of the change is to start the change so you need to start to start. In her book The 5 Second Rule, Mel Robbins says – just count down '5,4,3,2,1' and don't hesitate, just go, just start!

Start to Finish

Look around you and notice how much unfinished 'stuff' there is around you. For example-

- Unfinished work or home projects that take up physical space and are constant reminders of what you haven't got done.
- Unfinished conversations that are hanging in the air and need to be brought to closure for both parties to move on.
- Unfinished commitments that carry with them the guilt of knowing you have let someone, or yourself, down.

Now might be a good time to make a real effort to Start to Finish so look at what is unfinished and make a plan to close these things out. Close them either by doing them or even deciding that they don't need to be done and just closing them off so they aren't hanging over you. Have a go at completing the next Own Zone –

Own Zone Own Zone Own Zone Own Zone **Own Zone** Own Zone Own Zone Own Zone Own Zone

Stop and take a quick look around you and make a list of any unfinished stuff you can see.

For each unfinished item ask the following questions:
   Why did you not finish it?
   How does not having it finished affect you?

96

Do you need to finish it?
What can you decide to close now without finishing?

Is there a trend or pattern in the things that are unfinished?

How can you improve your level of finishing?

Own Zone Own Zone Own Zone Own Zone Own Zone Own Zone Own Zone Own Zone Own Zone Own Zone Own Zone Own Zone Own Zone

Start to say No

How many time have you not said 'No' and ended up resenting the fact that you said 'Yes'. So why say yes? People will often say 'Yes' to preserve a certain image and appear nice, friendly, professional etc.

What is preventing you from saying No to things that you don't want to do, don't need to do or even things that you shouldn't be doing at all. Is it to preserve an image, or fear of consequences of saying 'No', or uncertainty, or lack of confidence or just a habit?

It's important to use your common sense when saying 'No', there are some things where it would be great to say 'No' but unfortunately there are things that we just must do for our family, friends, clients, workmates or boss!

Remember the Professional No, discussed earlier. You could start to say 'No' in a gentle way by saying you can't do what is being asked now but you could do it at an alternative time. This 'not now but later' approach shows that your time is valuable and give you some level of control over how you spend your time and energy.

Own Zone Own Zone Own Zone Own Zone **Own Zone** Own Zone Own Zone Own Zone Own Zone

Do you use 'No' enough to protect your time?

If no - where could you start?

What benefit would it give you?

Own Zone Own Zone Own Zone Own Zone Own Zone Own Zone Own Zone Own Zone Own Zone Own Zone Own Zone Own Zone Own Zone

Start to take responsibility

The only person responsible for making the changes you want is you. It's important to take responsibility for your actions and decisions and to have comfort in doing so. It's easy to pass the responsibility to someone else and find someone else to blame for why you have failed. This type of thinking produces a downward, negative spiral from which no good can come for you.

Own Zone Own Zone Own Zone Own Zone **Own Zone** Own Zone Own Zone Own Zone Own Zone

Do you take full responsibility for your life and decisions?

If no -where could you start?

What benefit would it give you?

Own Zone Own Zone Own Zone Own Zone Own Zone Own Zone Own Zone Own Zone Own Zone Own Zone Own Zone Own Zone Own Zone

Start to take control

This follows on directly from taking responsibility. You must take full responsibility for what you have control over – use the DIP process that is mentioned earlier to identify where you have control. Start small and build up your control and notice the difference it makes to yourself and to how others perceive you.

It should be noted that taking control doesn't mean that you turn into a control freak – exactly the opposite in fact. Control freaks try to control everything and everyone but by taking control of yourself you become much more centred and can make the right decisions for you without trying to control everyone else.

Own Zone Own Zone Own Zone Own Zone **Own Zone** Own Zone Own Zone Own Zone Own Zone

Do you have control over your life and decisions?

If no -where could you start?

What benefit would it give you?

Own Zone Own Zone Own Zone Own Zone Own Zone Own Zone Own Zone Own Zone Own Zone Own Zone Own Zone Own Zone Own Zone

Start to keep the promises you make yourself

Promises are stronger than goals. They are much more personal and as such carry with them a level of commitment that is higher than that associated with goals.

Starting to keep promises made to yourself might seem to be a very selfish thing to do. It is interesting to perhaps look at it from the angle that if you can't keep commitments made to yourself, how can you possibly keep commitments you make to other people?

Own Zone Own Zone Own Zone Own Zone **Own Zone** Own Zone Own Zone Own Zone Own Zone

Do you keep promises you make to yourself?

Where could you start?

What benefit would it give you?

Own Zone Own Zone Own Zone Own Zone Own Zone Own Zone Own Zone Own Zone Own Zone Own Zone Own Zone Own Zone Own Zone

Start to believe in yourself

Whether you think you can or think that you can't, either way you are correct. Start to believe in your capacity to change, and build on that belief by gaining the small wins as mentioned earlier in the book. Be aware of the language you use and make sure that it is positive and grounded. Let go of the negative baggage and dump the 'rear-view mirror', the future is in front of you, not behind you.

If you start to believe that you can make the change then that is a great place to start from. You'll be looking for the evidence that you can do it and not the evidence that shows that you can't do it. Your awareness shifts and you filter information in a different way, focused on the positive and affirming.

Own Zone Own Zone Own Zone Own Zone **Own Zone** Own Zone Own Zone Own Zone Own Zone

How would you describe your level of self-belief?

What effect does it have on you personally?

What could you do to increase your level of self-belief?
What or who could help you do this?

Is there anything or anyone that stops you from having more self-belief?

Imagine what you could achieve if you had more self-belief.

102

Own Zone Own Zone Own Zone Own Zone Own Zone Own Zone Own Zone Own Zone Own Zone Own Zone Own Zone Own Zone Own Zone

Start to let go of the baggage

Baggage acts as an anchor to the past and as such either holds you back from moving forward or creates drag that slows your progress. Sometimes people don't even recognise their baggage because it has become 'part' of them.

The thinking behind *RISE UP!* is that most baggage is external to you and so you can make a start to dump it. This might not be an easy process and it might never be fully complete but have a look at the following Own Zone and have a go at answering the questions – you might just surprise yourself!

Own Zone Own Zone Own Zone Own Zone **Own Zone** Own Zone Own Zone Own Zone Own Zone

What is your baggage?

What does it cost you personally to drag it around or be anchored to it?

What's stopping you from letting it go?

What or who could help you to let go of your baggage?

If you were free of your baggage, what could you do?

Own Zone Own Zone Own Zone Own Zone Own Zone Own Zone Own Zone Own Zone Own Zone Own Zone Own Zone Own Zone Own Zone

Start to build things that you value in your life

The last section focused on starting to let go of your negative baggage so it makes sense to look at building up what you value in your life. These are the things, knowledge and relationships that you can use to guide and support your change.

When previously discussing the things that you are to Increase, many of these fall into the category of things that you value. Take the time now to look at what you really value in your life and how you might go about building more of what you value. The Own Zone will help you to structure your thinking on this area – remember the Own Zones are designed to help and challenge you. You can keep them private and work through them on your own or you can share them and get some feedback or input from other people that you trust.

Own Zone Own Zone Own Zone Own Zone **Own Zone** Own Zone Own Zone Own Zone Own Zone

What do you value in your life?

How does this affect what you do?

How can you build more of what you value into your life?

Own Zone Own Zone Own Zone Own Zone Own Zone Own Zone Own Zone Own Zone Own Zone Own Zone Own Zone Own Zone Own Zone

Start to hang out with the right people

You have the right to hang out with people who are positive, grounded, fun, enthusiastic and supportive. These are the type of authentic people who will support you. The first thing you need to do here is to identify who they might be and where they are.

People who don't value or respect you will have a negative effect on you and block or discourage you. Move away from people who have a negative influence on you. The Energy Vampires have already been mentioned – they definitely aren't the type of people you want to be hanging out with as they will suck all positivity and energy from you.

There can be a problem if you are your own source of negativity. Often the harshest critic you have is the little voice in your head, your inner critic. The difficulty here is that it is very hard to get away from yourself! Some of the sections in this chapter are aimed at reducing the volume and intensity of this inner critic.

Own Zone Own Zone Own Zone Own Zone **Own Zone** Own Zone Own Zone Own Zone Own Zone

Who do you hang out with the most?

How does they affect what you do?

What is your inner critic saying to you?

How does that affect what you do?

How can you build more positive influences into your life?

Own Zone Own Zone Own Zone Own Zone Own Zone Own Zone Own Zone Own Zone Own Zone Own Zone Own Zone Own Zone Own Zone

Start doing things for yourself

Clearing baggage, keeping promises, finishing the unfinished are all ways of quietening the negative power of the little voice in our head. The importance of self-talk was highlighted in the Chapter on Increase, one thing you can do for yourself is to manage your self-talk so that you are saying nice things about yourself to yourself! Maybe even give yourself 'permission' to do something nice for yourself so you feel better.

Think about what you do for yourself. What small rewards, nice things or 'me-time' do you allow yourself? Remember that the things that make you feel better don't have to be public, they don't have to cost anything and they don't have to be big. They just need to mean something positive to you.

Doing nice things for yourself is important for your self-care and can boost your energy, confidence and attitude. Don't overlook the importance of doing this – it can bring huge value to you and your change journey.

Own Zone Own Zone Own Zone Own Zone **Own Zone** Own Zone Own Zone Own Zone Own Zone

What are you doing for yourself?

How does this affect what you do?

List 5 things that you could do for yourself that would have a positive impact on you

When can you start?

Schedule out things you can do for yourself for the next week, aiming for at least 1 thing per day.

Own Zone Own Zone Own Zone Own Zone Own Zone Own Zone Own Zone Own Zone Own Zone Own Zone Own Zone Own Zone Own Zone

Personal comment

The decision to Start what you need is a huge step forward in your *RISE UP!* journey. When I began to really think about and make positive decisions on what I needed to Start, the energy to do so came with the decision.

It's a very forward facing stage of the *RISE UP!* process, that should bring with it rewards for you. I'll finish with a quote from Xi Jinping, the Chinese President, that he made when talking about China's future development but I feel it can be applied personally in that you have to Start being yourself and not try to be somebody else.

> **We cannot dress up other people's yesterdays**
> **as our own tomorrows.**
> **Xi Jinping**

What I'm going to START

No.	Action to be taken by me.	When will I start?	What will it Cost?	How will I do this?	When will I finish this?	What Support do I need?

Table 3: Identifying the START activities

Own Zone - Notes

Own Zone - Notes

Chapter V

E - Eliminate

Introduction

I have noticed that to Eliminate 'stuff' from my life-space does not come naturally to me. It's not that I'm a hoarder but there is a tendency to keep things as opposed to get rid of them! This part of the *RISE UP!* process was difficult until I saw the results. Now I find it much easier to Eliminate stuff and then move on.

To Eliminate requires a high level of courage as it is often easier to persevere with, rather than eliminate, what doesn't add any value or benefit to your life. However, if you can manage to identify small things that you can eliminate, you will gain the confidence and momentum to tackle the larger things.

In the Reduce chapter, you looked at reducing what might be blocking you from achieving the change you want. Here you are asked to go a step further and to identify what you can, and should, Eliminate from your life.

Eliminate

The origin of the word Eliminate is in Latin and it translates as to put something out over the threshold or boundary. You decide where the threshold or boundary is, then actively put what you don't want or need outside your boundary.

How can you go about eliminating things from your life-space? Here your mind-set has to be firmly set, even more so than in any of the other actions involved in *RISE UP!* The Elimination cannot be viewed as temporary or partial but full on and permanent and as such should show a real impact on your change.

Choosing what to Eliminate

When you looked at what you should Increase, one of the categories was focused on increasing what you value in your life. When considering what to Eliminate you can take the opposite perspective and decide to eliminate what doesn't add value in your life.

As mentioned above, Eliminate should be viewed as a conscious and permanent decision. There needs to be a very definite cut-off point that you have placed in your mind-set or physical space, setting boundaries for what you will no longer accept. This means having a clear definition of what you value and of who you are.

For Eliminate to work, a high level of thought must be put into it. It might be a good idea to go with your gut with some of the Eliminate actions and to more carefully consider others. Be mindful that sometime kneejerk reactions can be wrong!

Eliminating what adds no value

You should be looking at eliminating what adds no value, or what you add no value to. There may be a few categories such as:

- Wasteful activities – things you do that just absorb energy and time but add no real value to yourself nor anyone else.
- Things that add no value – these just take up physical space and are of no use at all.
- Limiting relationships – these are the relationships that drain your energy, time and spirit and have no benefit to you.
- Negative attitudes – such attitudes can create and maintain barriers to your progression and interfere with key relationships.

It's worth taking the time to uncover all the things, activities, relationships and attitudes that add no value but you are still carrying with you, then decide how you are going to eliminate them. The next Own Zone will force your thinking on this topic.

Own Zone Own Zone Own Zone Own Zone **Own Zone** Own Zone Own Zone Own Zone Own Zone

When looking at what to Eliminate, think about the following:

What boundaries will you set that will help you to Eliminate purposefully?

Identify some things you could Eliminate.

Identify some things that you should Eliminate.

Identify some things that you must Eliminate.

Own Zone Own Zone Own Zone Own Zone Own Zone Own Zone Own Zone Own Zone Own Zone Own Zone Own Zone Own Zone Own Zone

Barriers to Elimination

There are many barriers to the process of elimination. Some of the barriers are external such as commitments you have, while others are internal such as your belief system or fears. In some cases, the external barriers might make elimination very difficult, however even the act of recognising the barrier can be helpful in terms of managing it. This is particularly true in relation to your internal barriers.

When you look at the internal barriers, they can be classed as:

- Habits – the unthinking routine ways that you have behaved in the past.
- Un-noticed – the barriers that exist because you have never thought about their impact.
- Desensitisation – the barriers that have been in place for so long that they are now normal for you.
- Fear – the barriers that cause you fear.

Own Zone Own Zone Own Zone Own Zone **Own Zone** Own Zone Own Zone Own Zone Own Zone

Look at the internal barriers that prevent you from Eliminating negative or limiting things, thoughts or people from your life.

What habits have you got that block you from eliminating?

What have you started to notice as internal barriers that you haven't noticed before?

When you look at yourself – notice what you are putting up with, what has become your 'normal'?

What difference would eliminating the negative or limiting things, thoughts or people make to you as you journey through RISE UP! Revolution You?

Own Zone Own Zone Own Zone Own Zone Own Zone Own Zone Own Zone Own Zone Own Zone Own Zone Own Zone Own Zone Own Zone

The *RISE UP!* process is based on getting you to think about your situation and to make decisions regarding how you are going to move forward. When examining the barriers that prevent us from eliminating non-value add things from our lives, one of the most damaging and limiting barrier is fear.

Through dealing with the barriers, especially fear, your change process can gain huge momentum with the creation and freeing of energy and space, physically, mentally and emotionally. The next section looks at fear.

Fear

The subject of fear in change was touched on in the Introduction, but it makes sense to bring it up again here and to dig a bit deeper into it. Susan Jeffers in her book Feel the Fear and Do It Anyway outlines what people fear and it resonates with the core thinking behind the *RISE UP!* concept.

> **We fear beginnings; we fear endings.**
> **We fear changing; we fear 'staying stuck'.**
> **We fear success; we fear failure.**
> **We fear living; we fear dying.**
> **Susan Jeffers**

Many of the fear-related barriers are presented in the quotation, so what can you do about it?

One method is to look at three different scenarios. This literally allows you to face your fears.
- Take the worst possible outcome that could arise from dealing with what you fear and describe it in as much detail as possible.
- Then do the same looking at the best possible outcome.
- Finally look at the in-between outcome.

This forms the basis of the next Own Zone which you are encouraged to think about, complete and then re-examine.

Own Zone Own Zone Own Zone Own Zone **Own Zone** Own Zone Own Zone Own Zone Own Zone

You are to build three scenarios based on what could happen when you face your fears. For each fear, describe each scenario and its outcome in as much detail as possible.

Scenario 1: What is the worst possible outcome from dealing with your fear?

Scenario 2: What is the best possible outcome from dealing with your fear?

Scenario 3: What is the mid-ground outcome from dealing with your fear?
Now that you have written down the possible outcomes of dealing with your fears, how do you feel about tackling them?

Own Zone Own Zone Own Zone Own Zone Own Zone Own Zone Own Zone Own Zone Own Zone Own Zone Own Zone Own Zone Own Zone

Types of Fears

When looking at the types of fears associated with any change they typically fall into three categories

- Fear of failure – this is the fear that often springs to mind when looking at making a change. The niggling doubt that it might not work out and you look like a fool or have wasted your time.
- Fear of rejection – once you've made the change then it might affect how others see you and they reject you or the change that you have made.
- Fear of success – now that you've made the change and its worked, what else will be expected of you and can you live up to these new expectations from both yourself and others.

Impact of fear

The primary impact of fear is that it closes you off from the potential resources that you need to make the change such as having a positive mind-set, accessing and using your skills and relationships.

This closing off means that you may feel that you are:

- Stuck.
- Undervalued
- Unable

However, there is a second possible impact of fear – and this is the impulse to resist and fight. This is the response that you need to tap into as it can act as a driver to push you. This is the basis of the notion of Feel the Fear and do it anyway.

It's useful to feel the fear but not to let it stop you unless what you plan to do is dangerous! By analysing the fear and sorting out what the impact is really going to be, you can then choose to go ahead and work with it as a fuel as opposed to a barrier. The brief quote below captures this sentiment very well.

Remember that underlying all our fears
is a lack of trust in ourselves.
Susan Jeffers

Personal Comment

The ability to Eliminate what doesn't add value in your life-space can be very useful. I found it created a significant amount of both life-space and satisfaction. Using Eliminate required some self-confidence to start but it also increased the level of self-confidence that I had. It allowed me to set clear boundaries as to what I want and don't want in my life-space. It's definitely worth persevering with, even if it is difficult at the start.

Hopefully this Chapter has challenged you to look at what you can Eliminate and given you the push to start to Eliminate what doesn't add value to your life-space.

What I'm going to ELIMINATE

No.	Action to be taken by me.	When will I start?	What will it Cost?	How will I do this?	When will I finish this?	What Support do I need?

Table 4: Identifying the ELIMINATE activities

Own Zone - Notes

Own Zone - Notes

Chapter VI
U - Unload

Introduction

To be honest, once I looked at where I was spending my time and energy, I found that I was carrying a lot that was not mine. I had somehow just taken things, activities and people on, even though I had no responsibility for them. I had allowed my life-space to become filled with stuff that belonged to other people. It was time to Unload!

In this section, you will look at what you can Unload – these might be things that need to be done or relationships that need to be looked after but not necessarily by you!

Responsibility

Are you clear in terms of what you are responsible for? By now, it should be clear to you that you are responsible for yourself and your actions, there is no getting away from that! However, you need to ask yourself what your responsibilities are and how they line up with what you do.

As well as clearly understanding your responsibilities, it is important to recognise and understand what other's responsibilities are. In many cases, there can be a grey zone where your and their responsibilities become muddled and confused so the first thing you need to fix is to clear that confusion. The Own Zone pushes you to look at how clear you are on your own and other's responsibilities.

'The key is taking responsibility and initiative, deciding what your life is about and prioritising your life around the most important things.'
Stephen Covey

Own Zone Own Zone Own Zone Own Zone **Own Zone** Own Zone Own Zone Own Zone Own Zone

How clear are you on your responsibilities – the things that you and only you have to do or look after?

At home…..

In work…..

In the community……

In the family…..

Make a list of your main responsibilities – you can break this into daily, weekly and monthly zones.

Own Zone Own Zone Own Zone Own Zone Own Zone Own Zone Own Zone Own Zone Own Zone Own Zone Own Zone Own Zone Own Zone

Auditing your actions

To get a picture of what you can unload, the following categorisation of what you feel you have to do may be useful. List what you are currently doing, what is in your mind and diary in terms of what you plan to do in the month.

Critically examine each action and list them under 3 headings:

- What you *could* do – these are the first things to unload.

- What you should do – these need to be a priority for unloading to someone else.

- What you must do – these are your responsibility and should not be unloaded.

For this to work you need to be clear in terms of what you are responsible for and then to be ruthless in defining the *coulds* and *shoulds* you have listed, plus identifying who you can unload them to.

> **'Responsibilities fall heaviest on those
> willing to take the load'**
> **Heather Day**

It is important to say that when you unload onto someone else you need to be sure that they have the capability to do what is required to the right standard plus they need to have the capacity to fit it in with all their responsibilities. It is your responsibility to make sure that they understand fully what is being asked of them. By doing these things you are preventing the need for you to jump in later and save the day.

Obligations and Commitments

Your obligations and commitments are usually on the list of what you must do. Imagine how well you could do them if you unloaded some, most or all the 'stuff' that is not yours. As part of the *RISE UP!* process, you are creating time and energy for the important things in your life including your obligations and commitments.

You must have the capability and capacity to deliver on your obligations and commitments. Failure to deliver could mean that you need to undertake some development work to improve your capability or to manage your workflow better if you are over-committed and have no capacity.

The Unloadables

When you are clear about what your responsibilities are, you can start to see that there are certain activities, things and relationships that are unloadable. But there are habits and thought processes that can stop you from unloading such as:

- Always stepping in and taking over what others are doing because you don't trust them to do it quite as well as you could.
- Making the assumption that if you don't do it then no-one else will.

- An inability to hand over responsibility to others in case you will no longer be needed.
- A fear of letting people down and getting blamed for what goes wrong.

Own Zone Own Zone Own Zone Own Zone **Own Zone** Own Zone Own Zone Own Zone Own Zone

What habits do you have that lead you to taking on what is not your responsibility?

What effect does this have on your energy, time, health, wealth, relationships?

How would you go about reducing or removing the habits?

What would the benefit be to you?

What barriers might exist that would make it hard to change?

Identify the main habits you will change, and start. Notice the effect!

Own Zone Own Zone Own Zone Own Zone Own Zone Own Zone Own Zone Own Zone Own Zone Own Zone Own Zone Own Zone Own Zone

Standing up for yourself

When dealing with the 'unloadables', it may be the first time that you need to look at giving 'stuff' to other people and in some cases to do this you have to be assertive.

Assertiveness as a rights-based action where you are standing up for your own position without the intention of damaging the other people involved. Effectively you are respecting their rights.

In order to be assertive you need to be sure of your facts, have clarity around where responsibility lies and ensure that the people you are unloading to have both the capacity and the capability to carry out the task. This means you must be focused in terms of explaining what is involved, checking that the person understands and then leaving them to get on with it. If they are struggling, be supportive but don't take the responsibility back, be assertive and stand up for yourself!

Outsourcing

Businesses are familiar with out-sourcing, which allows them to reduce costs by transferring work to outside suppliers rather than doing the work in-house. Would out-sourcing be an option when you are looking to unload?

The first thing you need to do is to look at what you can unload by out-sourcing. These activities might be;
- What someone can do better than you.
- What you intensely dislike
- What you don't do very well.

- What drains your energy, time and motivation.

You will find that your level of comfort with outsourcing might not be very high at the start. The recommendation would be to start outsourcing with what causes you the most 'pain' so you will have a significant gain very quickly, or to start with some small 'stuff'. Don't outsource without first thinking about it, then when you have made a considered decision you have more chance of working within your preferred comfort level. As your success grows so too will your confidence and comfort.

Complete the Own Zone below which is designed to get you thinking about out-sourcing.

Own Zone Own Zone Own Zone Own Zone **Own Zone** Own Zone Own Zone Own Zone Own Zone

What can you unload through outsourcing?

Where or who can you outsource to?

What would the benefit of outsourcing be compared to the cost to you?

What would your main gain be from outsourcing?

What danger might arise from outsourcing? How can you reduce any such negative effect!

Own Zone Own Zone Own Zone Own Zone Own Zone Own Zone Own Zone Own Zone Own Zone Own Zone Own Zone Own Zone

Unloading is not dumping

This is a very short paragraph! Don't dump – it causes resentment and resistance. You need to be fair to yourself and the others in how and what you unload.

Personal Comment

What I have found when going through the Unload process was that my level of distraction went down. I was able to concentrate on what I had responsibility for and this made me more productive.

By unloading what wasn't mine in an assertive way, people were much less likely to try and load me with things that were in fact their responsibility. The effect of unloading was that my chance of getting loaded with what someone else was supposed to do, significantly reduced going forward.

But remember – unloading is not dumping!

What I'm going to UNLOAD

No.	Action to be taken by me.	When will I start?	What will it Cost?	How will I do this?	When will I finish this?	What Support do I need?

Table 5: Identifying the UNLOAD activities

Own Zone - Notes

Own Zone - Notes

Chapter VII
P - Park

Introduction

In this section, the focus will be on what you can Park. Identifying what needs to be done but not necessarily done immediately!

Pressure

The feeling of being overwhelmed is often because you have too much to do, you've overcommitted yourself in terms of your current resources. This creates pressure that can be paralysing, preventing you from both making decisions and taking action.

The ability to decide to Park some of the demands and be satisfied with the decision is one way to reduce pressure. With a reduction in pressure comes a clearer head and the ability to stand back, analyse the situation and then make the best decision on how to proceed. In other words, you take back a level of control in what you are doing and how you think about these things.

When you are feeling under pressure from your workload, relationships or life in general, using the thinking associated with Park can be useful.

Reasons to Park

The reasons to Park can be set out into 6 main categories as follows:

- Currently you can do nothing about the 'task' nor can you unload it.

- The task doesn't need to be done now.

- The resources are not available to do the task as they are tied up somewhere else. It can be useful to Park when you find that you don't have sufficient:
    o Time
    o Energy – both physical and emotional
    o Knowledge
    o Experience
    o Trust
    o Support
    o Permission
    o Money

- You don't want to do the task at this time and no-one else is depending on you to do it.

- The specific details of the task are not defined yet and your experience is that such tasks can either change or disappear.

- It won't negatively affect some other person or yourself in a harmful way if you don't do the task now.

You could use this as a checklist when you are considering if you can apply Park to a task or activity.

Own Zone Own Zone Own Zone Own Zone **Own Zone** Own Zone Own Zone Own Zone Own Zone

Look at your current list of what you intend to do now.

Using the 6 criteria outlined above, decide on what you can Park and mark it with a P.

What effect will Parking some of your list have on you in terms of saving your energy and time?

Proactive procrastination

When you look at everything in you are trying to do and to squeeze into your day, it's often useful to look at it from a 'not now' perspective.

This can be considered as Proactive Procrastination with the following characteristics:
- You can see what you have to do.
- You can decide on what to Park
- You have considered the impact of Parking
- You are balancing resources with demands
- Parking is not the same as abandoning
- You know exactly what you have parked and will not lose it
- You have every intention of dealing with what you have parked, in other words you are not dumping it.
- You have a time set for when you will return to it.

Imagine the feeling of control that you would have from applying this type of thinking to your obligations and commitments.

Your system for Parking

Your obligations are always there and as already said, Parking is not dumping but making a conscious decision not to so something now. This means that a system must be in place to allow you to capture, prioritise and schedule what you intend to Park.

Having such a system brings with it several advantages such as:

144

- Peace of mind, you aren't carrying loads of reminders and task details in your head. They are all captured in one place.
- Visualisation of what you must do and how much there is on your plate. Once you can see something then you can make the decision as to when you will do it.
- Being proactive and controlled in your approach to your obligations, not reactive and inconsistent.
- You can see where obligations are coming from – maybe allowing you to see where someone else is dumping their 'stuff' on you and taking advantage of your good nature!

There are many options available for your system, the most important thing is that it must suit you. Don't overcomplicate it, keep it as simple as possible. Your system might be a notebook that you make your lists in. It might be a diary where you schedule your tasks, it might be on your phone, tablet or laptop using something like OneNote. It doesn't matter what form it takes as long as it is:

- Portable.
- Simple.
- Doing the job in a way that suits you.
- Editable so you can change and move entries.
- Logical.
- Secure – if private or valuable information is in it.

But remember – the best system in the world will only work if you use it. Consistency in terms of capturing, prioritising and scheduling the tasks that you are putting into Park mode is essential.

Own Zone Own Zone Own Zone Own Zone **Own Zone** Own Zone Own Zone Own Zone Own Zone

What is your system going to look like?

What is your preference – paper based, electronic, a mix of both?

Decide on what you want to use and then start!

Own Zone Own Zone Own Zone Own Zone Own Zone Own Zone Own Zone Own Zone Own Zone Own Zone Own Zone Own Zone Own Zone

PORT and FORT

It is possible to weigh up the impact of Park by doing a very simple analysis. Take 2 sheets of paper, draw 2 lines on each sheet to divide them into 3 sections each.

Sheet 1 is PORT – focused on the impact of doing the 'task' in the Present by looking at and writing down:

- the Opportunities this might bring,
- the Risks associated with doing it now
- the Threats that could occur due to doing it now

Sheet 2 is FORT, focused on the impact of doing the 'task' in the Future, i.e. Parking it, where you identify and write down:

- the Opportunities that may present themselves by doing the 'task' in the future.
- the Risks associated with doing it in the future
- the Threats that could occur due to doing it in the future

This would give a very basic way to compare doing the task now or Parking it and leaving it until some future date. This structured approach can help you to decide on what to Park by looking at the impact.

Own Zone Own Zone Own Zone Own Zone **Own Zone** Own Zone Own Zone Own Zone Own Zone

Look at your task list and where you are unsure of whether to Park or not, then do your PORT / FORT analysis

Own Zone Own Zone Own Zone Own Zone Own Zone Own Zone Own Zone Own Zone Own Zone Own Zone Own Zone Own Zone Own Zone

Priorities and Park

Priority and park are two sides of the same coin – what has to be done now (your priority activities) and what can be done later (your activities that you can Park). What factors do you need to look at when considering and deciding on what has Priority?

Understanding the importance of the tasks you have to do is a much better way to prioritise than looking only at the urgency of the task. Importance focuses on the impact of getting the task done (or the consequence of not doing it!!), whereas Urgency is only concerned with time.

Another factor that needs to be considered is what can you actually fit in to your schedule now and what resources do you have access to – these would be classed as your capacity and your capability. When you have a shortage in either then the task cannot be completed without causing problems elsewhere.

The activities you give your time to tend not to exist in isolation, in many cases you need to look at the knock-on effects of doing versus parking. The 'dependency' factor can mean that if you Park one thing the knock-on effect could far outweigh any benefit you would get from parking.

Finally, if you have a clear idea of your responsibilities and take into consideration the priority factors then you can increase your level of focus and productivity by clearing what you must do now and have comfort in parking the rest.

Own Zone Own Zone Own Zone Own Zone **Own Zone** Own Zone Own Zone Own Zone Own Zone

How do you prioritise at present?

What drives your actions, urgency or importance?

If you made better decisions regarding setting your priorities what benefits would that give you?

Own Zone Own Zone Own Zone Own Zone Own Zone Own Zone Own Zone Own Zone Own Zone Own Zone Own Zone Own Zone Own Zone Own Zone

Park your phone

Think of what you could do if you parked your phone – even for a couple of hours a day. The curse of FOMO (Fear of Missing Out) regarding what's happening on Social Media has led to missing out on real social and productive activities!

Parking your phone could free up a significant portion of time every day, time that you could use for much better purposes than being on Facebook or Instagram.

149

Try it and see – you might surprise yourself, and not really miss anything at all!

Park v Unload

What is the difference between Park and Unload? In the last Chapter the emphasis was on determining what you could unload and the impact that might have. The essence of Unload is that you do not intend to take back what you have unloaded, you have effectively cleared it off your plate and it is now someone else's responsibility. It's not a case that you will be returning to do it later – what you Unload is not yours anymore.

The essence of Park is the realisation that there are things you must do but you don't need to do them now. You have the intention, indeed you have the need and responsibility, to return to them later and look after them. It's not a case of you won't do them, you still 'own' them, you just won't do them now.

Personal comment

The ability to prioritise what you must do now and Park what you can do later, can free up an incredible amount of time and energy. It is like Proactive Procrastination, where you decide and control what you are parking.

The most important thing is that you have control. I know that in my case, when I would have just put things off without any real thought, it tended to add to my stress instead of reducing it. However, using the more mindful and thoughtful approach involved in Park, I found that there was no stress as I had control. One of the main aims of the *RISE UP! Revolution You* approach is to have control over what you do.

I also found that it is important to have a good system for capturing what you are putting into Park mode. This capture system can't be your head, it must be a real system whether electronic or paper based, and it must suit the way that you work. I use the Bullet Journal method created by Ryder Carroll, it suits the way I work so I'd advise that you find a system that suits you – just remember to keep it simple and then Park will work for you.

What I'm going to PARK

No.	Action to be taken by me.	When will I start?	What will it Cost?	How will I do this?	When will I finish this?	What Support do I need?

Table 6: Identifying the PARK activities

Own Zone Own Zone Own Zone **Own Zone Notes** Own Zone Own Zone Own Zone

Own Zone Own Zone Own Zone **Own Zone Notes** Own Zone Own Zone Own Zone

Closing Comment

Now that you have come to the end of this book, I hope that you have enjoyed *RISE-UP! Revolution You*. I would be delighted to think that you have learned something of benefit to you, and even more delighted if you have learned something about yourself.

Change is a very personal journey, it differs for everyone in terms of where the start and end points are, what the hopes and ambitions are and when struggles and challenges are met along the way.

My own change journey started because of a traumatic, unexpected event but *RISE UP* has led me to a higher level of satisfaction, grounded-ness and even contentment.

I suppose what I have mostly learned on my journey is that it is essential to look for the real value and the affirming in everything that I do. But, more importantly, to never give up and always, always, keep the promises you make, especially those you make to yourself.

Thanks to everyone who has helped me.

All the best on your journey

Jim

Useful Resources

Some books that I found useful are listed below:

Roy F Baumeister & John Tierney
Willpower   ISBN 978-1-8461-4350-2

Jill Bolte-Taylor Ph.D.
My stroke of insight   ISBN-978-0-3409-8050-7

Jack Canfield
The Success Principles   ISBN 978-0-0071-9508-4
The Power of Focus   ISBN 978-0-0918-7650-8

Norman Doidge M.D.
The brain that changes itself   ISBN 978-0-1431-1310-2

Dwayne D. Dyer
Being in Balance   ISBN 978-1-4019-1068-6
The power of intention   ISBN 978-1-4019-0216-2

Charles Duhigg
The Power of Habit   ISBN 978-1-8479-4624-9

Andrea Hayes
My Life Goals Journal   ISBN 978-0-7171-7436-2

John Hegarty
Hegarty on Creativity.   ISBN-978-0500-51724-6

Dan Meredith
How to be F...king Awesome   ISBN 978-1-78133-188-0
I get Sh*t done   ISBN 978-1-78133-220-7

Tom Peters
Re-imagine!   ISBN 978-1-4053-1395-7

Tony Robbins
Awaken the giant within   ISBN 978-0-6717-9154-4
Unlimited power   ISBN 978-0-6848-4577-7

Dave Trott
One + One = Three   ISBN-978-1447-28703-2

Caroline Webb
How to have a good day   ISBN-978-1509-81824-2

Mel Robbins
The 5 second rule   ISBN-978-1-68261-238-5

Own Zone Own Zone Own Zone **Own Zone Notes** Own Zone Own Zone Own Zone